The A to Z Book of Cats

By Michael P. Earney

Copyright Michael P. Earney 2020 All Rights Reserved.
No part of this book may be reproduced, stored in a retrieval system, or transmitted
by any means, electronic, mechanical, photocopying, recording,
or otherwise, without written permission from the author.

ISBN-13:   978-1-941345-74-0   HB
ISBN-13:   978-1-941345-75-7   PB

Frontispiece by Elowen Sandidge-Earney, 10yrs old
Cover Illustration by Michael P. Earney
Alphacat Font by Michael P. Earney

Canyon Lake, TX
www.ErinGoBraghPublishing.com

Acknowledgments

Thank you to family and friends for their encouragement and support during the production of this book.

Special Thanks go to Kathleen's Graphics, whose tireless work with formatting always makes my books look great.

The Cat's Meow

There's lions and tigers and lynx
There's Siamese and Burmese and a cat named Sphynx
There's cute and cuddly with soft, tiny paws
Then there's fierce and savage with sharp, deadly claws
Just as pumas and leopards can tear you apart
A Kurilian bobtail plucks the strings of your heart.
While it's lovely to hear those soft, soothing purrs
It's best to remember, they are all carnivores
From panthers that threaten the ranchers' herds
To your little kitty endangering birds
While bobcats are shot as protection for sheep
The millions of birds killed, raises scarcely a peep
Of course, your house cat is precious to you
But, all of the big cats could use some love too
Cheetahs, the fastest mammals on land,
Like all of the wild cats, they sure need a hand
It's essential we keep their homes free and wide
In order to show them we're taking their side.
Cats, gone from the wild, would truly be sad
Leaving just cats, domestic, as all that we had.

Michael P. Earney 2019

The A to Z Book of Cats

The domestic cat has been around for a very long time, in fact, seeing how ingratiating cats are, I believe what is known as the house cat very likely started out as the cave cat. This book will cover not just the domestic cat but all of the cat family, Felidae and Panthera. Felis catus is the only member of the family felidae that is domesticated. TICA, The International Cat Association says there are 58 breeds, IPCBA, the International Progressive Cat Breeders Alliance lists 73, CFA, the Cat Fanciers Association, 44, FIF, the Fédération Internationale Féline 43. You might also see the claim that there are 100 different breeds of domestic cats in the world.

That being said, there are plenty of instances of cats such as cheetahs, lynxes and even lions and tigers, being raised by humans from a very early age or captive cats being tamed to the point where they share space with humans and can legitimately be called pets. It was long thought that the cat was domesticated by the ancient Egyptians, they were after all, an important part of Egyptian life for more than 30 centuries. We have all seen those mummified cats that accompanied there owners to the grave, but it is now known that cats were tamed thousands of years earlier. Where they were first domesticated and exactly how long ago may never be known.

Spayed females live 62% longer and neutered males live twice as long as their intact family members. This is rather a mixed blessing, if the thought of losing your kitty makes you sad, getting it fixed will postpone the inevitable somewhat. On the other hand, while there may be less cats, those that are alive will be around longer to continue to prey on birds and other wildlife. It is estimated that in the UK alone there are 64.8 million bird deaths annually due to cat predation. In the US it is believed that the feral cat population, estimated at 25-60 million, kills several billion birds per year. The 73 million pet cats take their toll too. This is of grave concern to the Audubon Society and other wildlife groups and should concern us all. Unfortunately, domestic cats usually only kill birds in "play", they don't need the extra food. The pet food industry whose income was $24.6 billion in 2016 is expected to be $30.1 billion in 2022 in the US alone. There is no doubt that a domestic cat adds an important dimension to life for many people that other pets may not, however, in our increasingly populated world responsible ownership is increasingly important. Which, in a way, brings us to the big cats. The big cats, depending on who you ask, are those belonging to the genus, Panthera, these are; Lion, Leopard, Tiger, Jaguar, Leopard and Snow Leopard. Some include under this heading; the mainland Clouded Leopard and the Sunda Clouded Leopard. All are threatened by habitat loss, poaching and human-wildlife conflict. In other words, they're having to make room for us. The tiger, lion, leopard and jaguar are all endangered species. Smaller wildcats include; the cheetah, bobcat, jaguarundi, ocelot, lynx and caracal. Then all of the increasingly smaller cats down to the rusty-spotted cat that will fit in your hand, all threatened to some degree or another. The title of smallest cat in the world goes to; the South African Black footed cat (Felis nigripes), The Rusty-spotted cat (Prionailuros rubiginosus) and the Kodkod (Leopardus guigna), found in South America. Take your pick. If you ever owned a cat you know how unique and special they can be while at the same time retaining that essential quality that sets cats apart.

> A German Shepherd, a Doberman and a cat died. In Heaven all three faced God who wanted to know what they believed.
>
> The German Shepherd said. "I believe in discipline, training and loyalty to my master."
>
> "Good!" said God. "Come sit by my right side."
>
> "Doberman, what do you believe?"
>
> The Doberman answered. "I believe in the love, care and protection of my master."
>
> "Aha!" said God. "You may sit to my left." Then God looked at the cat and asked, "And what do you believe?"
>
> The cat replied, "I believe you are sitting in my chair.

Throughout the book you will find drawings and paintings that were created during two classes I gave at El Progreso Memorial Public Library in Uvalde, TX. in the summer of

2019. The children who attended were aged from 7-12 yrs. I thought it would be interesting to see if there might possibly be any that I could use in the book I had started. The five pictures selected by an independent panel of judges are included, as are many of their other wonderful works.

A. is for Abyssinian.

The Abyssinian cat is said to originate in Egypt, genetic evidence shows that it came from the coastal regions of India and parts of South East Asia. British and Dutch traders brought them to Europe in the 1800's. The one shown at the Crystal Palace Cat Show in 1871 was said to have been imported from Abyssinia so, from then on the breed was called, Abyssinian. Similar to the Panama Hat. The Abyssinian is a short-haired with a distinctive "ticking", each hair of its tabby coat is banded with different colors, which is best appreciated during grooming. Cross breeding has given rise to other colors, blue, fawn and silver while retaining the distinctive "tick". Abyssinians are a popular pet but, if you decide to get one you should be prepared to spend a lot of time with it. They love to play; you'll be busy finding toys to keep them amused. They love to jump and climb as high as they can. They will retrieve endlessly, just like a Labrador retriever and will walk on a leash, just like a dog. Abyssinians have a natural curiosity and abundant energy and don't like being left alone. This means you might come home to a bit of a wreck if you leave them too long. They are devoted and attention grabbing. If you are house bound, this might be the cat for you.

Cool Fact: The two world wars almost wiped out the Abyssinian in Europe. Luckily, its popularity had led to it being bred in Canada and the USA so, new Abyssinians were imported. Then in the 1960s they were decimated again in England by feline leukemia. Once again, Abyssinians were brought in and the breed was re-established.

What other cat names start with A?

B. Is for Bobcat.

The Bobcat, (Lynx rufus) with subspecies, is the most common wildcat in North America. It's slightly smaller than its cousin the Lynx which it closely resembles, both have the short, bobbed tail. Once heavily hunted for its fur, there are now laws in place to protect it and all spotted cats. Consequently, the bobcat is returning to much of its previous territory which stretches from southern Canada down into Mexico with unconfirmed reports of sightings in remote areas of Guatemala. This means that the bobcat is happy in a wide range of habitats, from mountains and forests to brush land and desert. Males scent mark their territory, generally 25-30 square miles, for females it's about 5 sq. miles. The bobcats' shelter, known as its natal den, might be a cave or under a rock or in a hollow log, this will be supplemented with shelter dens, similarly protected places where it can stay if it's off hunting far from home. Bobcat kittens are usually born in the spring. Litters of up to 6 kittens is normal. Their mother kicks them out of her territory when they are 8-11 months old. Bobcats eat 3-4 lbs of meat per day; rabbits, rodents, deer, even birds and bats which they can leap into the air to catch. They are not above eating fish and a Bobcat has been seen catching a shark! Ranch animals offer an easy meal which brings them into conflict with farmers and ranchers who consider them a predator to be shot. Hunting and trapping of bobcats is permitted. A program of tracking, capturing and collaring bobcats provides important data that will help develop a protection and management strategy for the future.

Cool Fact: Most of the bobcat's hunting is done at night. A mirror like membrane, the tapetum, just behind the bobcat's retina, reflects light allowing it to use low light both on its way in and on its way out.

What other cat names start with B?

C Cheetah

C. is for Cheetah

The Cheetah, once roamed throughout Africa and much of Asia. *Acinonyx jacabatus*, has the largest remaining numbers and are found in North, South and East Africa. The North East and South East African cheetah are closely related. There is also the North West Africa cheetah. The subspecies, *A. venaticus* is found in Iran, it is the only remaining cheetah in Asia. fewer than 50 are thought to survive. They are listed as, critically endangered, as is the North West species. All the others are listed as vulnerable by the IUCN, the International Union for Conservation of Nature. The dry forests, scrub-lands and savannahs they inhabit are disappearing; poaching, the illegal pet trade and the usual lethal interface with humans is taking its toll. The King cheetah, with three stripes down its back and large, blotchy spots was thought to be a separate species, it was eventually determined that a mutant gene was responsible for Kings appearing among commoners. What sets the cheetah apart from its relatives, a divergence that may have happened 6.5 million years ago, is its light, streamlined and extremely agile body which, together with rough foot pads, claws that don't completely retract, that provide great traction, long back legs and a few other distinctive features, makes it the fastest mammal on land. How fast? It can go from zero to 60mph in 3 seconds. Run at 40mph with short bursts of 70mph. The cheetah's ability to rapidly change direction, helped by its tail which is used like a rudder, increases its success rate. Cheetahs are easily tamed, the ancient Egyptians and Chinese emperors kept them as pets and for hunting. In Medieval Europe cheetahs got to ride on the back of horses to assist in the hunt.

Cool Fact: In *Alice's Adventures in Wonderland* when the Cheshire cat fades away, leaving only its face, we read; "Well! I've often seen a cat without a grin," thought Alice, "but a grin without a cat! It's the most curious thing I ever saw in my life!"

What other cat names start with C

D

Devon Rex

D. is for Devon Rex

Devonshire, Dorsetshire, and Cornwall are the west counties of England. Cornwall is the westernmost, where England sticks its big toe into the Atlantic. Cornwall seems inaccessibly remote to many British while Devon is considered the English Riviera. It was in Devon where a stray cat gave birth to an odd curly-haired kitten. Beryl Cox who was caring for the stray, raised the kitten which became the father of a new breed, the Devon Rex. That was in 1959. Although it resembles the Cornish Rex, each was the result of a different gene mutation. The Devon is unusual in having very little guard hair. Cats have three types of hair, guard hair, awn hair and down hair. (the Cornish Rex has only down hair.) In spite of, or perhaps because of its unusual look, the short curly coat, big eyes, large, low set ears, turned up nose, curly whiskers, slim body, long legs and unusually large paws, the Devon has become a popular breed. Called "pixie cats", "alien cats", or "a monkey in a cat suit" they endear themselves to those they choose to buddy with. A lot like the Abyssinian, Devons like to climb, they are intelligent, like to play and interact. Clowning and entertaining, for which they expect even more attention, is to be expected. Their sparse coat, which shouldn't be brushed, means Devons are always looking for warmth. But, the fact that they like to get under the covers with you may just as likely be because they love people; family, friends, kids, and strangers. Devons are generally healthy but are prone to certain health problems. From being a stray, the Devon has now won over people on both sides of the Atlantic.

Cool Fact: In Devon and the other cider producing counties, wassail, a hot mulled cider, was drunk around the winter solstice to celebrate the apple harvest and to ask the gods for a good harvest in the coming year.

What other cat names start with D?

E. Is for Egyptian

The Egyptian word for cat is, mau, myw or meow. Calling a cat by the sound it makes, may seem simplistic but, things were simpler 5000 years ago. Or were they? Those pyramids are pretty complex. They didn't call dogs 'woof', but, iwiw, which is what they heard when dogs barked. There is the Egyptian Mau cat and Egyptian cats that are not maus. Maus are the only naturally spotted domestic cat. Because of the strict rules governing cat breeds, a mau found in Egypt wouldn't meet the exacting breed standards. The actual breed, Egyptian Mau, was not named until two Egyptian Tabby cats that were the progeny of two that had been mated in Italy, were taken to the USA where they formed the base of the breed, Egyptian Mau, in 1956. Confused? The Egyptians have been great fans of cats for centuries. they particularly liked the way cats took care of the rodent population. Being an agricultural based civilization, storing grain was of paramount importance. Keeping vermin out was a big challenge, met by the cat population. Cats can be seen in murals painted on the walls of ancient temples, there are cat sculptures and cat mummies,(300,000 cat mummies were found when the temple of Bastet, the cat goddess, was excavated).The festival honoring Bastet was the largest and most popular celebrated in all of Egypt. It was prescribed that lioness goddesses be appeased with "feasts of drunkeness," Although Bastet was originally depicted as a lioness she was later changed into a domestic cat. As you can see, cats were very highly regarded. The penalty for killing a cat was severe. The distinctive M on tabbies' foreheads is said to represent the sacred scarab beetle, the mark left by the prophet Muhammad after he stroked a mau or, could be... 10 year old, Alicia Teague's drawing received honorable mention. Valentina Vileri, 8 years old, drew the other cat.

Cool Fact: Research suggests that the great Sphinx of Giza that has the body of a lion and the head of a Pharoah is much older than previously thought and that it originally had the head of a lion.

What other cat names start with E?

F

FLAT-HEADED CAT

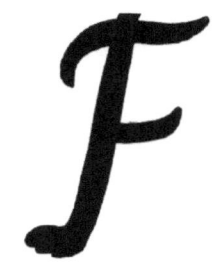

F. is for Flat-headed cat *Prionailurus planiceps*

The Flat-headed cat lives along rivers and streams in Malaysia, Sumatra, So. Thailand and Borneo it has a short tail and is about the size of an average domestic cat. Its small, rounded ears that are set low on its head, do not protrude above its skull. Compared to other cats its head is elongated and flattened. It has short legs, long narrow feet, that are more webbed than the Fishing cat. Like the Fishing cat and the Cheetah, its claws are not fully retractable. Eyes that are closer together and farther forward that regular cats, makes finding and catching water dwelling creatures easier. With teeth that are designed for seizing and gripping slippery prey it will come as no surprise to learn that it eats mostly fish, frogs and crustaceans. It is thought to hunt at night frequenting any body of water where it will frolic and play. It has no problem swimming under water. Once they have a fish or a frog, they will carry it some distance from the water's edge, just in case it should flip back in the water. They are rather like a raccoon in that they feel around in the mud in search of food and again, like a raccoon, will 'wash' things that they find. Being rare and elusive, little is known about its breeding habits or much else, for that matter. It is known that the males have a range of around 20sq. miles, females only about 2sq. miles. We do know that the Flat-headed cat is on the IUCN threatened species Red list as Endangered. Waterways tend to be exploited by humans which puts the Flat-headed cats' habitat at risk. As so often happens, we barely know of a creature's existence before it's in danger of disappearing. Many species are in danger of extinction or have become extinct before we even know they exist.

Cool Fact: Two flat-headed cats were observed by zoologists in the Berbak National Park in Sumatra. The park officers had never seen or heard of the species. That was in 1995. It was 1996 before the first photograph of a Flat-headed cat in the wild was ever taken.

What other cat names start with F?

G. is for Geoffroy's Cat *Leopardus geoffroyi*

Geoffroy's cat is native to Argentina, Uruguay, So. Chile and the Bolivian Andes where it can be found at altitudes of 3500m. or 11000ft. Much of what I have written about the flat-headed cat is true for the Geoffroy's, it's about the size of a domestic cat, it's spotted with a relatively short black-tipped tail, there is a melanistic variety, it's found mostly in wetland and forested areas. The Geoffroy's is also a good swimmer, preferring fish to birds which has earned it the name 'fish cat' but it's also known as 'gato de montes' or mountain cat. However, it lives on the opposite side of the world from the flat-headed and is considered to be fairly common. But its status is not that well known and as with all the wild cats, the impact of habitat lose and poaching is taking a toll. However, the Geoffroy's seems to be adapting better than some and is utilizing the areas where man has changed the landscape. The Geoffroy is often mistaken for the Southern Tiger cat or Tigrina, *L. guttulus,* as their territories overlap and they do interbreed, creating hybridized versions of the two. Other small, spotted cats in South America like the Pampas, the Kodkod and the Fishing cat lead to more misidentification. Still, the chances of seeing any one of them is slim as they mostly hunt at night.

Cool Fact: Etienne Geoffroy Saint-Hilaire, 1772-1844 was a French naturalist who's view that species alter over time, ridiculed and dismissed during his time, was finally vindicated in the 20th century. In 1796 he wrote: It seems that nature is confined within certain limits and has formed living beings with only one single plan, essentially the same in principle, but that she has produced variations in a thousand ways in all her accessory parts. If we consider one class of animals in particular, it is there especially that her plan will be most evident: we will find that the divergent forms under which she was pleased to make each species to exist all derive from one another.

What other cat names start with G?

H. is for Highlander

The Highlander is a USA breed created in 1993 and was known as the Highlander Lynx, being a hybrid of the Jungle Curl and the Desert Lynx. In 2004 TICA insisted on the name change, (the lynx part sounded too 'wild' for their liking), and in 2008 accepted the Highlander as a Preliminary New Breed. The Highlander can come in short hair, long hair, short tail or long tail, have extra toes and the ears, that curl over in the first two weeks after birth, don't always curl. It could take a few generations for breeders to get the Highlander 'look' perfect. That being said, it's a medium to large cat, males weigh 15-20lbs. females 10-14lbs. They are gentle, playful, intelligent and inquisitive. They are also very sociable, so they need a lot of your time and attention. Highlanders like to play in the water and swim. They might even jump in the bath with you! They will want to be your best friend to the extent that they are not adverse to learning to walk on a leash and take a stroll in the park with you. Crossing breeds can cause some health problems but, so far the Highlander appears to be free of any. Which is good news being that as such a rare breed, buying a kitten could set you back a thousand dollar or more.

Cool Fact: A Highlanders ears that don't curl over will be longer than a regular domestic cat's, being inherited from the Desert Lynx side of the family.

What other cat name begins with H?

Iberian Lynx

I. is for Iberian Lynx *Lynx pardinus*

The Iberian Lynx is native to the Iberian Peninsula, it's another animal on the IUCN Red list as Endangered. Iberia, as the peninsula is commonly known, is made up mostly of Spain and Portugal but includes Andora and small parts of France. The usual problems, overhunting, poaching and habitat fragmentation took their toll on the animal but, in addition, the population of its almost exclusive prey, the European rabbit, plummeted due to myxomatosis and another infectious disease, which had been introduced into France in order to lower the rabbit population. This left the Lynx with very little to eat. There were only about one hundred of the cats left when the 21st century started. Thanks to some pretty drastic conservation efforts which included; restocking the rabbit, improving habitat, re-location and the introduction of Iberian lynxes raised in captivity, by 2012 there were 326 cats out in the wild. Habitat preservation, rabbit population management and monitoring of their population will hopefully, lead to continued increase in their recovery. Of course, once you mess with Mother Nature you are going to have to keep up the effort to turn things around. Climate change, the Lynx is not handling that too well, inbreeding due to restricted area of habitat and shortage of mates doesn't help. Road kills are the leading cause of unnatural death. Competition for prey comes from the Red fox, the Egyptian mongoose and the Wildcat. The Iberian lynx does hunt all of the above plus the common genet, a cat-like animal introduced from Africa about a thousand years ago. Also quail, which they can grab out of the air but, rabbit is still their most favorite of all.

Cool Fact: The Algarve, on Portugal's Atlantic coast, is the most popular tourist destination in Portugal, drawing over four million visitors a year. It's also very popular with birders, being the first landfall for birds migrating from Africa. Oh, yes, it's where you will find Portugal's Iberian lynx population, too.

What other cat names start with I?

J

Jaguar

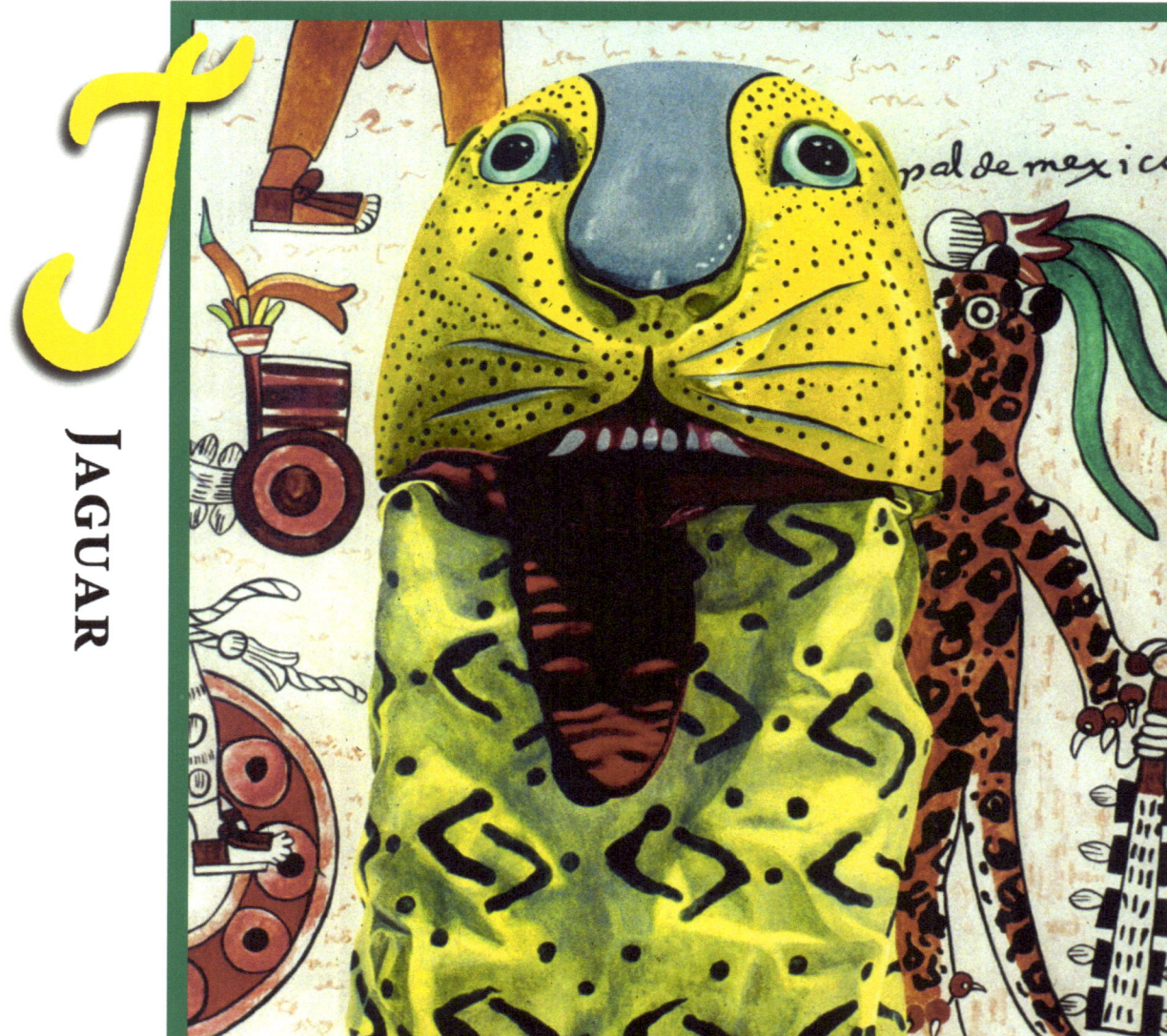

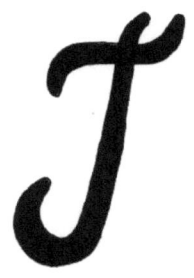

J is for Jaguar *Panthera onca*

The Jaguar is the only one of the world's big cats found in the Americas. 25"-30" at the shoulders it is the largest feline in the Americas. The Jaguar originated in North America and spread down to Paraguay and Argentina. Brazil has the largest population, mostly in the Amazon basin. The Brazilian rain forest receives 33" of rain each year. It absorbs solar radiation and 40% of carbon dioxide in the air. It is feared that this amazing resource and its jaguars may disappear. The home of what may be the last Jaguar in Arizona is threatened by a proposed copper mine that will destroy thousands of acres of critical habitat. There are believed to be 15,000 left in the wild putting it in the Near Threatened category. The Jaguar was once seen as a god in Peru, Mexico and Guatemala. Aztec and Mayan rulers wore Jaguar skins, their thrones were covered in Jaguar skins and when they went to war their warriors wore Jaguar skins. Jaguars were depicted in paintings, sculpture and pottery. All parts of the jaguar were used in royal ceremonies, (kings were even buried with skins, claws and fangs). Jaguar comes from the Tupi-Guarani *yaguara*- "he who kills with one leap." The Mayan name, *Balam* referred to the Jaguar in the context of "brave warrior." Even today the jaguar, now called *el tigre,* can be seen in popular rituals and fiestas. In certain villages, young men dressed as Jaguars, fight each other with the intent to spill blood so that the Jaguar deity will send rain for the crops. Illustration from Earney's "Magic Faces. Caras Magicas" a book of Mexican mask paintings with text in English and Spanish.

Cool Fact: Costa Rica has the most Jaguars in Central America and most of them reside in Corcovado National Park. Biologists there, wanting to lure Jaguars to their camera in order to study them, found that an after shave lotion, Obsession for Men ®, drew them when none other would.

What other cat names start with J?

K is for Khao Manee

Khao Manee meaning "White gem" or Khao plort meaning "Complete white" is a naturally occurring white cat originating in Thailand. The Khao Manee was revered for centuries by the Thai nobility. It was thought to bring good luck. Given that the Siamese cat is so popular, it is somewhat of a surprise that the first Khao Manee only arrived in the USA in 1999. Once it was adopted by Western breeders, it quickly made it to "Advanced New Breed." The Khao exhibits features that commonly affect white cats, it will often have odd eyes, one will be blue the other another color such as green or gold. They are also, unfortunately, either hearing impaired or completely deaf. It is still quite rare in the west but, those that have them know that they are vocal, active, inquisitive, intelligent, can be naughty, need company and like to snuggle.

The Thai word for cat is another of those onomatopoeic words, like we saw with the Egyptian Mao, in this case it is, Maeo. In the 14th century a book of poems called, *Tamra Maew*, or *Tamra Maeo*, appeared in Thailand. Versions dating from the 19th century still exist. It has illustrations of cats and is believed to have been a cat breed guide. Apparently, they are working on translation of the poems.

"The cat's meow", like, "the cat's pajamas" is an expression from the 1920's it denotes stylishness, impressive or attention getting qualities. Cats' meow to get your attention. They are saying; "Hello, look at me." So, something that grabs your attention is, "The cat's meow".

Cool Fact: Some cats do not meow.

What other cat names start with K?

L. Is for Lion *Panthera leo*

The lion has symbolized Strength, Fierceness, Power and nobility for thousands of years although it is only the second largest cat in the world, the tiger being first. From depictions in caves dated to 17,000 years ago, through lion-headed gods and goddesses in sculptures and carvings down to our day, the lion rules. It's no accident that the British Royal coat of arms includes a lion. The lion represents England, a unicorn represents Scotland. One of England's kings was called, Richard the Lionheart. Many thousands of years ago there were gigantic lions in Europe and North America, perhaps in South America too, down as far as Patagonia. Now there are only the African and Asian lion and they are listed on the IUCN Red list as vulnerable due to habitat loss and us. Still big game hunting is very popular (the fact that you might be the one to shoot the very last lion seems to appeal to some people). Feared and revered, male lions can weigh up to 550lbs., 250kg. With its prominent mane and its muscular body, lions, and lionesses for that matter, present a challenge that hunters find irresistible. A pride of lions consists of a few males, several females and their young. Females do most of the hunting and male lions generally hunt alone. The CECIL ACT (H.R.2245) seeks to protect wildlife and extend the Endangered Species Act, it is named for Cecil the lion, killed in 2015 by an American trophy hunter.

The animated film *The Lion King* produced in 1994 had songs by Elton John and Tim Rice. It was the highest grossing film of 1994. That version led to other derived works, the Broadway adaptation being perhaps the best known. The story bears similarities to William Shakespeare's *Hamlet*.

Cool Fact: Zebras just look gray to Lions.

What other cat names start with L?

M Manx

Nonpedigree — Gregorio

Jakob Flores
Manx Cat

M is for Manx

Manx cats are a breed of domestic cat that come from the Isle of Man which sits between England and Ireland in the Irish Sea. The Manx is best known for its complete lack of a tail, which makes it a "rumpy" or a short, "stumpy" tail. The "longy" can also occur. Though the Isle of Man has been populated since before 6500BC, it's not known when this naturally occurring mutation came about. It is the "rumpy" feature that sets it apart from other cats, that, and its elongated hind legs and rounded head. The Manx, which is quite rare, is sometimes called, the dog-cat since it has something of a dog's temperament. It will walk on a leash and accepts training. Due to its long hind legs, it runs like a hare. We had one in my father's bake house when I was a kid, for the same reason Farmers and Ships Captains liked them; they're skilled hunters. Manx syndrome, a spinal condition that affects Manx cats, is almost always Spina Bifida, which can happen to any breed of cat and to humans. Whether Manx syndrome is unique from Spina Bifida has yet to be determined. However, the spinal disease that plagues the Manx breed, has convinced some British breeders that the Manx should be allowed to die out. Since the Manx has spread throughout the world and readily breeds with other cats, that's not likely to happen. 8 year old, Gregorio Jimenez and Jakob Flores drew the illustrations.

The Isle of Man T.T. Competition, an annual motorcycle event, is considered to be the most dangerous sporting event in the world.

Cool Fact: Stimpy, of the animated series *The Ren and Stimpy Show* is a Manx cat.

What other cat name starts with M?

N

Norwegian Forest Cat

Norwegian Forest Cat

The Norwegian Forest Cat, known as a "Wegie" for short, is big and burly and like its wild ancestors with their long, thick double layered coat can handle cold winter months outside with no problem. In fact, its woolly undercoat reaches full density at that time of the year. Which means it can go climb trees even in the snow. Its extraordinary claws make it easy to scale rocks and trees. The Norwegian Forest Cat breed wasn't fully developed until the 1970's so it can't claim direct descent from those earlier cats. From antiquity the wild Norwegian Forest Cat played a dominant role in Nordic fables and were kept on Norwegian farms to keep the farmers' harvests free of rodents. Still, today's cat, independent, a good hunter of meat and fish, liking human company *and* open spaces, would look a lot like those ancestors if you were able to go back in time.

The illustration is by Emily Alderson, 12yrs. Emily's drawing doesn't show the silver tabby coat and almond shaped green eyes but, her delicate drawing was selected for first place when the pictures were judged at El Progreso library in Uvalde.

Cool Fact: One Nordic fable has Thor lose a contest of strength to the tricky god Jormundgard disguised as a skogkatt, (forest cat). The skogkatt was a "large long-haired mountain-dwelling fairy cat". Sound familiar?

What other cat names start with N?

O Ocelot

O is for Ocelot *Leopardus pardalis*
(from the Aztec, tlalocelot)

Ten million years ago the ocelot and other small cats branched off from a lynx-like creature. While some of these descendants occupy very limited areas, the ocelot spread throughout the Americas. There are Ocelots on the island of Trinidad, whether they are a sub-species has yet to be determined. They once ranged as far as Arkansas and Louisiana. Along with the Jaguar and Jaguarundi, they are still occasionally seen in Texas, Arizona and New Mexico. Though not on the endangered list, a border wall would isolate those on this side and they would likely die out. The sub-species *Leopardus pardalis albescens* is endangered, fewer than sixty remain. They roam between Texas and Mexico and are likely to die out for the same reason. Twice the size of a domestic cat, it is second only to the jaguar. Ocelots are solitary hunters, hunting at night and sleeping during the day. They are picky eaters, removing the fur or feathers from their prey before eating. If they get full before they have eaten everything, they will hide what's left and come back for it later. Various environmental and wildlife rescue groups are working to protect this animal, you can do your bit by reducing your carbon footprint, shopping responsibly and opposing a border wall.

The cut-out, life size Ocelot is one of a series that includes headboards and folding screens.

Cool Fact: The painter Salvador Dali had a pet ocelot that he once took to a restaurant in New York City. When asked what it was he replied that it was only a cat he had painted with an op-art design.

What other cat names start with O?

Puma

P is for Puma *Puma concolor*

The name Puma comes from Quechua, the language of the Inca, it means, powerful. Its other names include; panther, cougar, mountain lion, catamount, mountain cat and, cool cat. Its wide range, from the Canadian Yukon to the Southern Andes in South America, is part of the reason for its many names. It is the largest mammal in the western hemisphere and the fourth largest cat in the world. The puma can be up to 15ft. in length and can jump 18ft. Still, the puma is classed as a "small cat" as they don't roar, it's related to the much smaller jaguarundi and purrs. Entirely exterminated from eastern North America except for *Puma concolor coryi* the Florida Panther. Once found in Texas and throughout the So. East the Florida panther is now confined to the Florida swamps where it is endangered due to habitat loss and fragmentation. Their biggest threat is heavy road traffic.

The puma's diet includes deer, elk and coyotes down to insects and rodents. Although they can swim, they don't like getting wet. This doesn't keep them from attacking alligators and eating them. New born cubs have spots which fade away at about 6 months. Mothers care for and nurse their young until they are about a year old. 18-20 years is the average life span.

This illustration is from the collection of Earney's cutout folding screens.

Cool Fact: The Puma holds the Guinness Book of Records for the animal with the most names. Over forty in English alone.

What other cat names start with P?

QUEEN

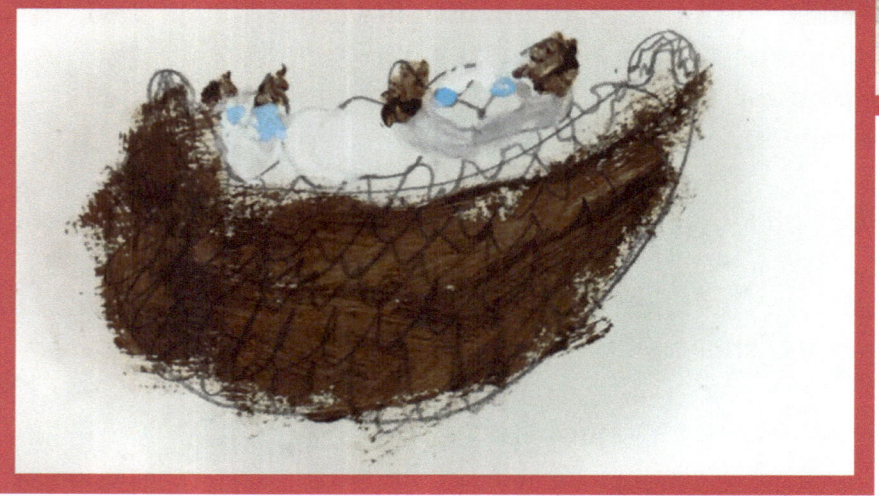

Q is for Queen

A pregnant cat is known as a queen cat and the process of giving birth is called queening. If you don't provide a queening box she will seek out a warm, comfortable, safe place. Even if you do set up a queening box she might still decide that she prefers your laundry basket instead. Labor can last as long as six hours. Queen cats can usually handle the process without help and since many kittens are born at night you may not be available anyway. As soon as a kitten is born the mother removes the membrane and licks the kitten clean. Although born blind, kittens quickly figure out where to suckle. Their eyes open after about seven days. The queen will be reluctant to leave her kittens but she will need a litter box, as in, somewhere to poop, and food and water. While nursing she will require at least three times more food than usual. It will be about two weeks before the kittens are fully mobile and are ready for solid food. After about ten to twelve weeks they will be ready to leave their mother and set out on their own.

9 year old, Natalie Goggins' queen cat might be a little hard to make out while 8yr. old Celise Castillo's playdoh sculpture queen, named Earthea, has ten eggs named, Snowball, Diamond, Rivers, Flames, Ice cube, Leaf, Twig, Shadow, Sandy and Sunny.

Cool Fact: Superfecundation. Female cats release more than one egg at a time and may mate with more than one male. This can result in a litter sired by more than one father. That's superfecundation.

Litter 1. A conveyance carried by men or animals.
      2. The young produced at one birth by a multiparous animal.
      3. Carelessly discarded waste materials or scrap.

Kitty Litter, now a multi-million-dollar business, was invented in 1947 by Edward Lowe. It was Fuller's Earth, a clay that typically consists of polygorskite or bentonite.

R is for Reed Cat *Felis chaus*
Jungle cat, Swamp cat

The Reed Cat is a medium sized cat, with its long legs it is the largest of the *Felis* species. Native to the Middle East, South and Southeast Asia, southern China and the subcontinent of India. It is mostly found in wetlands, swamps and dense vegetation. Listed as of Least concern on the IUCN Red list it is nevertheless, threatened by loss of wetlands, trapping and poisoning. While the kittens start out stripped and spotted, the adult Reed Cat has a uniformly sandy, reddish brown or gray fur though some males retain the dark rings on their forelegs. Melanistic, (black) and albino individuals also occur. It hunts birds, rodents, squirrels, hares, juvenile wild pigs, frogs and reptiles. Following the usual pattern of cats, it is a solitary hunter and maintains its territory by scent marking and urine spray. Reed Cats hunt throughout the day jumping high to catch birds and swimming to catch fish. Unusual for cats, it eats fruit too. Still, they like to take a siesta in the heat of the day. Even though the Reed cat is listed 'of least concern', covering such a wide area as they do, circumstances vary greatly. In addition, three subspecies are recognized and in some of the countries where the cat occurs, they have become extremely rare and are considered critically endangered. Hunting is prohibited in Cambodia, Laos and Vietnam but elsewhere they receive no legal protection.

Cool Fact: The Ring-tailed cat, found in Texas and the Southwest down to Veracruz in Mexico, is not a cat, despite its appearance, but a member of the Raccoon family.

What other cat names start with R?

S is for Serval *Leptailurus serval*

The Serval is native to Africa, though now rare in North Africa it is widespread in sub-Sahara. Slender, with a small head, large ears and short, black-tipped tail, its spotted and striped golden yellow to buff body helps the serval to blend in with the dry grasses of the wooded areas where it lives. It does not frequent the rain forest regions. Servals have the sharpest hearing in the feline world and the longest legs relative to its body size of any other cat. The serval's white spotted, closely set ears can rotate up to 180 degrees independently of each other. That feature and its long legs make for a very efficient hunter. It can leap over six feet in the air for birds and detect the slightest movement of its other prey, rodents, frogs, reptiles and insects. Servals are solitary hunters, mostly in the evening, at night and early morning.

Of Least Concern on the IUCN Red list the serval appears to be relatively safe. Adult males have body lengths of 2.7 feet and weigh in at 26lbs. Some people keep servals as pets but, they really need zoo-like conditions given their size, they need raw meat similar to what they would kill in the wild, they have a life span of twenty two years, ownership requires permits, is illegal in some places and, they are wild animals.

Cool Fact: The first Savannah cat was born in 1986, a hybrid of a serval and a domestic cat. Larger than a typical domestic cat Savannahs have the coat pattern of the original father while retaining the tameness of the mother.

Lorena Auguste brought her niece Lourdes to the library for the art class and decided to join in. She painted the Serval featured here.

What other cat names start with S?

Tiger

T is for Tiger *Panthera tigris*

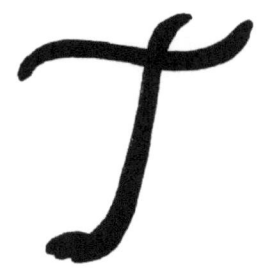

The Bengal Tiger is the subspecies with the most living individuals, it has 2500 by last count. There are nine subspecies. The Bali tiger was killed off in the 1940s. The Caspian tiger was last seen in the wild in the 1970s. The Indochinese has some 350 left. The illegal demand for tiger body parts, for use in Traditional Chinese medicine, has resulted in 75% of the Vietnamese population having been poached. The Javan has not been seen since 1979. The Malayan, the second smallest of the subspecies, has 500 left. The Siberian tiger living in remote parts, unlike the rest of the subspecies that live in some of the most heavily populated part of the planet, is doing okay. The Chinese government banned the killing of the South China tiger in 1977 though it is possible that it was already extinct at that time. There are 59 in captivity, not enough for the subspecies to survive. The Sumatran tiger, smallest of all the subspecies, is found only on the island of Sumatra. There are an estimated 400 to 500. It too is on its way to extinction due to habitat loss but, they are also being shot. So, things don't look good for the tiger. However, between 2010 and 2014, the tiger population nearly doubled. We should also mention there are White tigers and Golden tigers. The gene that produces white tigers has to be carried by both parents and occurs only once in 10,000 births. The Golden tiger is the result of another recessive gene. 11 year old Layla Gonzalez received 2nd place for her illustration.

Cool Fact: Unlike lions where the male always eats first, male tigers will let the female and cubs feed before joining in to eat like a family.

What other cat names starts with T?

Tyger Tyger, burning bright
In the forests of the night;
What immortal hand or eye,
Could frame thy fearful symmetry?
First verse of the poem by William Blake published in 1794

URAL REX

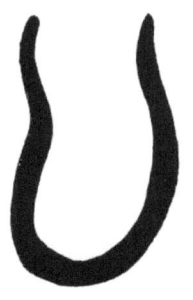

U is for Ural Rex

The rather odd looking fur of the Ural Rex is a natural mutation. There are records of free roaming domestic Ural Rex cats dating back to the 1940s. Nobody thought about breeding them until someone in Yekaterinburg, the 4th largest city in Russia, located in the Urals, mated a male named Vasiliy with his mother, a litter was born in 1994. More careful breeding was carried out and no genetic defects have been detected. The Ural Rex was recognized as a breed by the World Cat Federation (WCF) in 2006 and is fast growing in popularity. Vasiliy had a coat of tightly curled hair, almost like the cornrows some fashion conscious ladies favor. There are now short hair and longhair Urals of many different coat colors, with rows that are not so pronounced, eye colors can be of any kind and don't necessarily bear any relationship to the coat color.

The Urals is the common name for the Ural mountains and the area surrounding them. The mountains, one of the oldest mountain ranges in the world, run through Russia from the Arctic to Kazakhstan. The Lynx is the only wild cat found there. Polecats are there but the polecat is not a member of the cat family. For years Plutonium mines have dumped radioactive waste in the mountain's rivers and lakes, Uranium processing plant accidents have further polluted the heavily mined area.

Cool Fact: All of the Rex cats, the Dorset, the Devon, etc. have curly hair. Rex (King) comes from a 19th century Belgium King who kept curly coated rabbits.

What other cat names starts with U?

V is for Variety

Clearly, there is a wide variety of cats in the world and clearly, they play a large role in our history. From revered as gods in Egypt, important crew members on ships, the subject of countless stories, poems, sayings and superstitions they have been subjected to much love and great hatred. In the Middle Ages, the cat, after centuries of being loved and revered, became the symbol of evil to the Christian Church. Perhaps, because of its having been a pagan divinity, by the middle of the 13th century it became the personification of Witches. Once the Inquisition got going, cats were fair game. The most infamous example of cat hate was the festival of St. John. In many cities throughout Europe, on June 24th, crates of cats were hoisted to church towers then thrown down to the crowds below to be burned. This war on cats meant that there were insufficient of them to kill the rats that just then were carrying bubonic fleas. The result was that two-thirds of the population of Europe died of the Plague. The love of cats has resulted in works of art in many fields. The opera, *L'enfant et les sortilèges* by Maurice Ravel with a libretto by Colette, another cat lover, has a duet for two cats. Freddy Mercury of the group Queen dedicated his album, *Mr. Bad Guy* to his cats and the song *Delilah* to his cat Delilah. The musical *Cats* based on T.S. Elliot's *Old Possum's Book of Practical Cats* ran for 21 years in its first London production and the Broadway production ran for 18 years, now we have a film version. Maneki- Neko, the beckoning cat of Japan is traditionally a calico Japanese Bobtail but comes in every size, shape, color and material from miniature to large statues. Illustrations by Lourdes Auguste (2), Hikari Fleming, Jolee Olson and 11 year old, Kari Chapa.

Cool Fact: A Chinese legend says that once cats ruled the world. Tiring of the responsibilities they handed the job over to the next evolved creature, human beings. Since that time the cat has enjoyed a life of leisure and play.

W is for Wirehair

Also known as the American Wirehair, the Wirehair came about as a spontaneous mutation. Their springy coat is also dense, course and not exactly pleasant to touch. So, if you can't stroke your cat, what's left? Well, they are an indoor cat that is playful, intelligent, affectionate to their owners, (always hoping for some petting, perhaps) friendly toward children and other pets you might have while being quite independent and hardy. Though their fur may be abrasive their personality is not. They are not clingy, they're cats, after all but, they seem to tune into their owners feelings and will offer support and comfort if you need a little TLC. Aside from the hard to miss curly coat, the other dominant features are; high cheekbones on a rounded head, blue, amber or gold eyes, sometimes there will be a mix, one of each. The wirehair originated in upstate New York in the mid-1960's. It's ranked as the most rare of the forty one Cat Fanciers Association breeds. They are also very popular so, if you think you might like one, a kitten could set you back $800.00 to $1000.00

As with humans, one of the most common health problems that can plague your cat is obesity. Each breed has its own appropriate weight so try to keep it there. Prevention is the best way to stay healthy, for your cat and for you.

> As I was going to St. Ives
> I met a man with seven wives
> The seven wives had seven sacks
> Every sack had seven cats
> Every cat had seven kits
> Kits, cats, sacks and wives
> How many were going to St. Ives?

Cool Fact: The riddling poem above may have been inspired by an Egyptian papyrus that features, cats, mice and a sequence of sevens. **How many cat names start with W?**

X stands for Extinct

X stands for Extinct

X'd out. Gone. Lost forever. None left. Extinction is forever and while we understand that the Saber-toothed tiger, along with the dinosaurs disappeared millions of years ago, extinctions are happening today too. The disappearance of species that are happening now are due almost entirely to what mankind is doing to the planet. It seems as though just about everything we do has an adverse effect on other creatures, the land, water and air. Sometimes deliberately, often by accident but always because there are more and more of us and less and less of them and our needs outweigh all else. The balance of nature has been upset to such a degree that, just as Alexander von Humboldt pointed out at the end of the 18th century, it may be too late for it to recover. Unfortunately, our love of pets only adds to the problem. In the USA alone there are more than 73 million pet cats, millions more feral cats, pet dogs and all kinds of other pets. The business of feeding, caring for and maintenance of a pet only adds to the impact on nature and those species that depend upon it. Just remember, that includes us too. Even though we like to think we can get along without all that wild stuff out there, we can't. Third place Saber-tooth Tiger by Jonathan Cantu.

The National Geographic Society Organization funds projects aimed at saving big cats at the same time as big game hunters pay huge amounts in order to be able to shoot them. As we see elsewhere in this book, cats are killed for their bones, teeth and fur. Many other organizations work to protect the environment from destruction and help nature to recover. We all have to do what we can to lessen our footprint by being more aware, consuming less and speaking out against waste and ill-conceived projects that are making things worse.

Cool Fact: A cat's purr helps it to heal any broken bones or fractures it might have. Animal therapists have concluded that sick humans heal quicker with a purring cat around. Why those purr vibrations are good for you is still a mystery.

Y York Chocolate

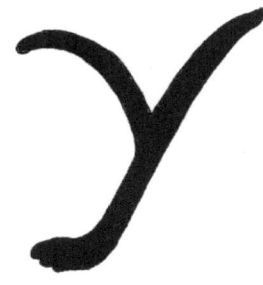

Y is for York Chocolate

Speaking of extinctions, the York Chocolate presents an interesting case. The breed was established in 1983 in New York State by Janet Chiefari through some incestuous inbreeding. It is considered a show cat but is only recognized by the WFC in Germany. In 2016 the breed was considered extinct! Wikipedia writes about it in the past tense although there are owners out there who have not gotten the message yet. Certainly, it is uncommon to rare. A kitten, should you find one, will cost $600.00 - $1000.00

They are or were, I don't have any up to date information, long haired, fluffy, solid chocolate, lilac, some say lavender, or with some white. Some have a combination of all three. Almond shaped eyes that are either green or gold. They are a large, affectionate, sweet, loyal, intelligent and curious cat. They are kid friendly and very talkative. They enjoy being petted, cuddled and held though they can be shy. Being that they are very good hunters, you will have to spend time with them playing active games to keep them from going out after birds. Since the York Chocolate became popular in parts of Europe, it's possible that should they disappear from the States, somewhere in the world, the breed will continue. Shorthair by 9yr. old Conner Cantu received 4th place.

> Pussy cat pussy cat where have you been?
> I've been to London to visit the Queen
> Pussy cat pussy cat what did you there?
> I frightened a little mouse under her chair.

Cool Fact: Just because we don't know about them doesn't mean they don't exist. A little spotted cat, *Leopardus guttulus,* was discovered in 2013 in Southern Brazil. It hasn't been given a common name yet. Native indigenous people living in the rain forest may have a name for it, if only someone would ask them.

What other cat names start with Y?

Z stands for Zoonosis

Zoonoses are animal diseases that can be transmitted to humans. An infection or parasitic disease contracted from your pet is called a zoonosis. Cat bites and scratches may carry bacteria and cause infection. Cat scratch fever is caused by an as yet unidentified bacterium. Washing and antiseptics will work for ordinary bites or scratches but if the offending cat is showing abnormal behavior it should be checked for rabies and anyone attacked by a rabid cat needs immediate post exposure immunization. Delay could be fatal. It is worth remembering that in our normal every day interaction mites, fleas and fungi can be transferred. Cats should be checked and treated regularly for fleas. Scalp ringworm, a fungal infection, can be caused by cats. An allergic reaction is usually due to dander in a cat's fur. Asthmatic attacks and even hives can result from dander. Cat boxes, cat feces and feces contaminated soil should be disposed of carefully and though we rarely think about it, petting a cat, touching its bedding, dishes or toys is best followed by hand washing. Good hygiene for you and your cat will protect you both from transmittable diseases but watch out for that sandbox in the playground, it's likely used by stray cats, carrying who knows what. Illustrations by Mylee Olson, 9 year old, Luke Packer, and Angela Villanueva.

Cool Fact: Most cats don't like being bathed but they spend nearly half of their waking hours grooming. It's not just in order to look good, their saliva contains enzymes that are a natural antibiotic that guards any wounds from infection. That rough tongue stimulates blood flow improving circulation. Grooming themselves and each other is relaxing and helps to keep fleas and dander from interfering with any petting or cuddles it might get from you.

Bonus Cat: Leopard

An A to Z book of cats wouldn't be complete without the leopard so, since the lion took the L spot, (the lion's share is the greatest or best part of the whole) the leopard is our bonus cat.

The leopard, the smallest of the big cats is the most geographically widespread. There are many subspecies.

The Amur leopard is native to Russia and northern China it is critically endangered on the IUCN Red list.

The African is found in many African countries. It is the one we think of when we visualize a leopard.

The Anatolian also called the Russian or Asian was thought to be extinct having not been seen since 1974. In 2015 a carcass found in Turkey was identified as an Anatolian. Let's hope that wasn't the last.

Persian. Also known as the Caucasian they roam the mountains of Iran. Three Persian leopards released into the Russian Caucasus State Nature Biosphere Reserve appear to be breeding and increasing.

Arabian. Listed as Critically Endangered by IUCN, found in Saudi Arabia, Yemen and Oman.

Indian. Widely distributed, India, Nepal, Bhutan and parts of Pakistan. Listed as Vulnerable by IUCN as populations decline.

Indochinese. Southeast Asia and southern China. Disappearing due to deforestation and poaching.

North Chinese. Listed as Endangered by IUCN.

Javan. Found only on the island of Java. IUCN Critically Endangered.

Sri Lankan. Indigenous to the island of Sri Lanka. Endangered.

Sinai. No current record of these in the wild. Possibly extinct.

Zanzibar. Possibly extinct.

Snow Leopard. Mountains of Central and South Asia. Vulnerable.

Clouded Leopard. Himalayan foothills into Southern China. Vulnerable. The clouded has the most interesting coat of all the leopards, it's a kind of mixture of stripes and spots.

The Formosan clouded was declared extinct in 2013 but there was an alleged sighting in 2019. Just as we have seen with the other big cats elsewhere, things don't look good for wild cats or for most other things in the wild.

The leopard Illustrations are from Earneys' cutout headboard collection and 11 year old, Kaitlyn Rodriguez.

While I hate to finish on a down note, it can't be emphasized too much that the natural world is undergoing great stress caused, for the most part, by Mankind. We have the duty and responsibility to do all that we can as individuals to protect nature. Our place in the fabric of life on this planet is as precarious as every other part of the whole, we can and must do all we can to hold this great tapestry together.

Cool Fact: The Dewclaw is a vestigial digit, claw or hoof on the foot of certain mammals. So called because it only reaches to the dewy grasses in the ground.

The Owl and the Pussy-cat went to sea
In a beautiful pea-green boat,
They took some honey, and plenty of money.
Wrapped up in a five-pound note.
The Owl looked up to the stars above,
And sang to a small guitar,
'O lovely Pussy! O Pussy, my love,
What a beautiful Pussy you are,
You are
You are!
What a beautiful Pussy you are!'
Pussy said to the Owl, 'You elegant fowl!
How charmingly sweet you sing!
O let us be married! too long we have tarried:
But what shall we do for a ring?'
They sailed away, for a year and a day,
To the land where the Bong-tree grows
And there in a wood a Piggy-wig stood
With a ring at the end of his nose,
His nose,
His nose,
With a ring at the end of his nose.
'Dear Pig, are you willing to sell for one shilling
Your ring?' Said the Piggy, 'I will.'
So they took it away, and were married next day
By the Turkey who lives on the hill.
They dined on mince, and slices of quince,
Which they ate with a runcible spoon;
And hand in hand, on the edge of the sand,
They danced by the light of the moon,
The moon,
The moon,
They danced by the light of the moon.
Edward Lear (1812 - 1888)

More A to Z Cats

A. American shorthair
B. Balinese, Burmese, Bengal
C. Chinchilla, Caracal, Colocolo
D. Donskoy
E. Exotic Shorthair, European wildcat
F. Foldex
G. German Rex
H. Havana Brown, Himalayan
I.
J. Javanese, Japanese Bobtail
K. Korat, Kashmir, Kinkalow
L. LaPerm, Lykoi, Leopard cat
M. Munchkin, Margay, Minskin
N. Nebelung, Napolean
O. Ocicat, Oriental Oncilla
P. Peterbald, Persian, Pixie-bob
Q.
R. Ragamuffin, Russian Blue, Ragdoll
S. Snowshoe, Scotish Fold, Selkirk Rex
T. Tiffany, Toyger, Tonkinese
U. Ukranian Levkoy
V.
W. Wila Krungthep
X.
Y.
Z.

Bibliography

Telesco, Patricia. *Cat Magic*. Destiny Books 1999

Conrad, Barnaby. *Le Chats de Paris*. Chronicle Books 1996

Cubitt, Gerald S. *Portraits of the African Wild*. Prion Press 1993

Edney, Andrew. *ASPCA Complete Cat Care Manual*. 1992

Readers Digest Illustrated Book of Cats. 1992

The Complete Cat Breed Book. DK Books 2013

Morris, William. *American Heritage Dictionary*. Houghton Miflin Co.

International Cat Care, icatcare.com

Animal Planet

Wikipedia

Shutterstock

Reviews: If you enjoyed this book, Michael P. Earney would appreciate it if you would leave a review on Amazon, Goodreads, or any other Review site you like.

Also, don't forget to tell your friends! Word of mouth advertising is the most precious ***"Thank You"*** a reader can ever give an author.

About the Author: Michael P. Earney is a fine arts painter who grew up in England. His writer's voice reflects curiosity and passion for the world of nature. His text is instructive yet playful. The illustrations are executed with grace and fine detail. Earney is in his element as artist, writer, educator, and naturalist. To learn more about this author's books and various achievements please visit his websites.

Contact Mr. Earney: themichaelearney@yahoo.com
Websites: www.MichaelEarney.com and www.earneyworks.com
Publisher: www.ErinGoBraghPublishing.com/authors/mearney
Books on Indie Lector: www.indielector.store/michael-earney.aspx

www.ingramcontent.com/pod-product-compliance
Lightning Source LLC
Chambersburg PA
CBHW042030150426
43199CB00002B/16